SKY'S ALL WRINKLED

Bil Keane

FAWCETT GOLD MEDAL • NEW YORK

The Family Circus
© 1991 Bil Keane, Inc.
Dist. by KING FEATURES SYNDICATE, Inc.

A Fawcett Gold Medal Book
Published by Ballantine Books
 Published in the United States by Ballantine Books, a division of Random House, Inc., New York, and simultaneously in Canada by Random House of Canada Limited, Toronto.

Library of Congress Catalog Card Number: 91-92199

ISBN 0-449-14620-0

Manufactured in the United States of America

First Edition: December 1991

"Oh, PJ! You're a real bottle of laughs!"

"But if it doesn't snow, how is Barbie s'posed to ski?"

"I bet you could kick a football a long way with wooden shoes."

"Can I go to Claire's party? She handed me an imitation!"

"We do NOT put play money in the collection basket."

"I bet my shadow would be good at basketball."

"Mommy! Come quick! PJ just had a disaster!"

"If a witch flew on that broom,
two kids could sit on the back."

"Mommy! The pot's losing its temper."

"I guess I'm not letter-perfect."

"How do you divide your love among four children?"

"I don't divide it. I multiply it."

"Will you talk it to me, Daddy?"

"Grandma, are your teeth true or false?"

"How 'bout that! Trees in umbrella stands!"

"Our Father who art in heaven
Halloween thy name..."

"Candles are old-fashioned. Let's wire him for electricity."

"I know why Cinderella wore glass slippers. So her toes could see out."

"I wanna get rid of the cold, but I wish I could keep this deep voice."

"It has a pocket for my head."

"Dolly's school would be better if they didn't have that lady up front talkin' all the time."

"That bathtub looks like the
Persian Gulf."

"Tangerines are smart. They divide themselves up into bite-size pieces."

"But, Daddy! Horses don't run out of gas!"

"I said 'maybe' and that's final!"

"Submarines are just boats that sink on purpose."

"Was it a REAL shoe or did the Disney people build it?"

"There's a new rule for Show-and-Tell. No more bugs."

"Know what I weigh? Three-oh inches!"

"You say 'boys will be boys' when Billy and Jeffy do something. How 'bout 'girls will be girls'?"

"Mommy, a nightgown isn't the same as an evening gown, is it?"

"How do you get your legs to stretch so far?"

"After you die God plays back all your sins on videotape."

"Daddy, will you move the sun, please?"

"Why do I have to keep writin' in these K's when they don't make any noise anyway?"

"Cameras shrink us so Grandma can
carry us around in her wallet."

"I wish we could have GRUEL for breakfast. Oliver Twist even wanted seconds."

"I don't know what time the party's over, Mommy, but you can come about nine and hang around."

"I've heard that story before."
"Who read it to you, Mommy?"

"I want to talk to Grandma, but PJ won't stop hugging her."

"Let's find one about
a non-smoker."

"Can Jason stay over? His mother works."

"I fell on the slidewalk!"

"My left leg weighs 'zactly the same as my right leg."

“What else did I do that was funny when I was little?”

"You have to learn numbers so you can telephone people."

"Behold! It snoweth!"

"God gift-wrapped the world!"

"I hate that. Mommy's giving our clothing sizes to somebody for Christmas."

"Mommy, when we finish these lists will you send the tape to Santa Claus?"

"If you can't find Billy just call Santa. He knows where everyone is."

"He's been studying for hours.
I've never seen him
concentrate so hard."

"Betcha Jesus missed out on a ton of presents 'cause his birthday and Christmas were on the very same day."

"Who invented 'ho-ho-ho'?
Santa Claus or the
Jolly Green Giant?"

"Jeffy tried to kiss Santa's ring."

"Every year you say you're going to address Christmas cards on summer vacation, but you never do."

"You don't have a fireplace, Grandma, so how 'bout hanging your stocking by the thermostat?"

"I remember Dopey, Grumpy, Sneezy and Doc, but what are the names of your OTHER elves?"

"29 cents just to send it across the street?"

"Grandma came through!"

"Listen! I thought I heard eight tiny reindeer!"

"They won't know it till they're grown, but their BEST gifts are the memories they're making."

"Choose one thing, Jeffy. You can't take all your presents to bed with you."

"The mailman's busy season is over and now it's the trashman's."

"Good night, Albert, g'night, Freddy,
g'night, Arnold, good night..."

"Mommy's watching her weight...
in the mirror."

"If you won't let me stay up, will you blow this for me at midnight?"

"Nite, Daddy! See you NEXT YEAR!"

"Hey! The puddles have all been laminated!"

"If Mother Hubbard only had a dog, why did they call her Mother?"

"I'm still sleepin' inside."

"Mind if I suggest a better spot
for your snowman?"

"I want to make this heart full of love, but I don't know how to draw it."

WHO PUT TEETH MARKS INTO ALL THESE CHOCOLATES DADDY GAVE ME?
NOT ME
BIL KEANE

"Not me!" "Not me!"

"We'll eat in the kitchen. I think the dining room table has been rezoned."

"Call me Mother Nature. I made a snowflake!"

"I'm watching with Bonnie."

"When we have kids Grandma won't be just GRAND. She'll be GREAT!"

"They all ran after the farmer's wife! She cut off their tails with a carving knife!"

"Not a 'false alarm,' Jeffy —
a WRONG NUMBER!"

"Hitch yourself up, Daddy!"

"Somebody's growing cigarettes in that sand!"

"Three things with horns are..
the devil, a car...and
Hagar the Horrible."

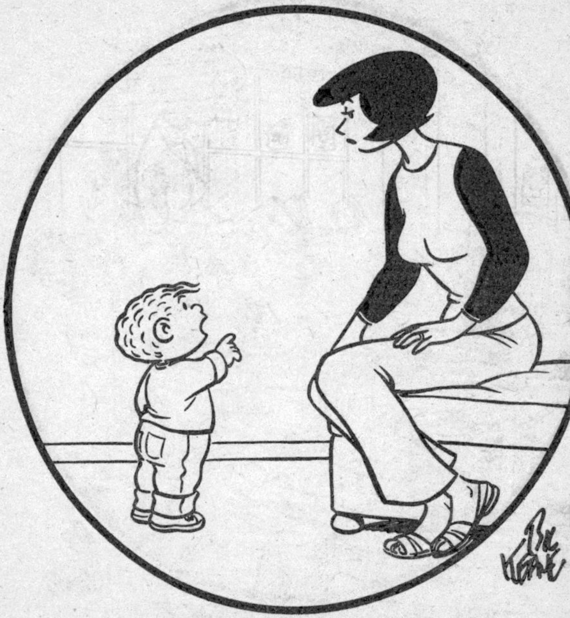

"How could a little bird tell you?
Little birds can't talk.
They chirp."

"That's Daddy's place, PJ! He's the chairman of dinner."

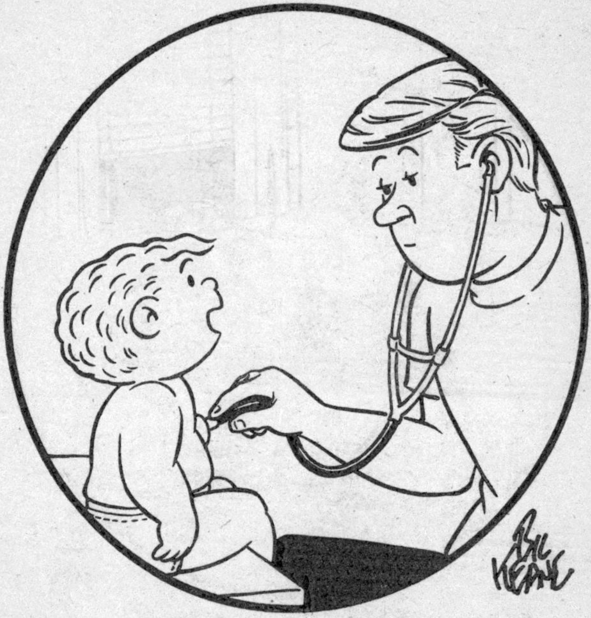

"How do I sound in stereo?"

"My teddy bear doesn't HAVE to talk.
We have ESP."

"Merrily, merrily, merrily, merrily,
life is but a scream!"

"Why should I hate girls?
I'm a girl."

"Could the snake really talk, or
was it like one of the Muppets?"

"Adverbs are used to mortify adjectives."

"I know who you are — Mr. BADwrench!"

"I've been exercising for years
and didn't know it."

"How do you know it's junk mail
before you open it?"

"If we had an intercom system, you could read us all to sleep at the same time."

"I got a ONE on my report card!
It's for 'days absent.'"

"You're CHICKEN, Jeffy!"

"You're my kind of man, PJ. Hard head and soft heart."

"Mommy, tell Billy to stop puttin' the cap back on the toothpaste every time."

"I'll bet Jeffy would flunk the cherry-tree quiz."

"Jeffy! You're letting all the germs get away!"

"Read a story that will give me ideas for a good dream."

"That's okay if it bleeds, Mommy. There's a lot more blood where that came from."

"Did you know we live on a PLANET?"

"Jeffy's eating with his mouth full."

"It's a butterfly coming out of
its cartoon."

"Why do bears hyperventilate in the winter?"

"I'll show you how I can dance, Grandma. You sit down and clap."

"Whenever I have a cold I forget what everything tastes like."

"Thank goodness Leap Year Day comes only once every four years."

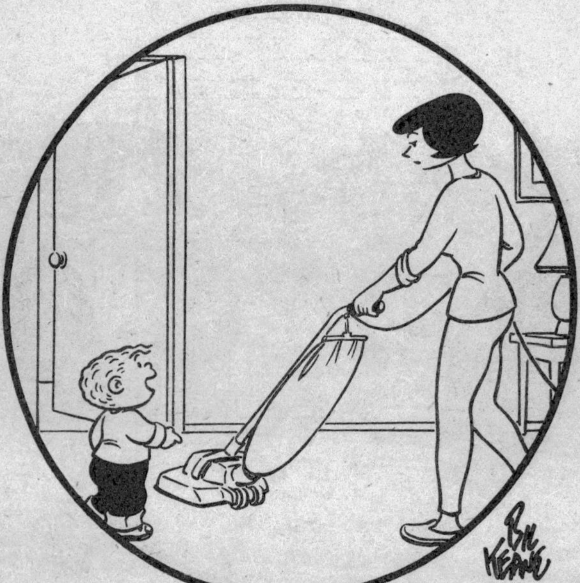

"Can I help you mow the carpet?"

"If Grandma is in her twilight years you must be at daybreak."

"It's a 24-hour flu, so you'll be up in, let's see...exactly 14 hours."

"Grandma said, 'Simmer down!'
What's simmer?"

"Daddy, how do you keep from tripping when you walk?"

"Look! A piece of moon!"

"I don't want to hear you call 'Mommy' anymore!"

"Thel! I'm thirsty!"

"Mommy! Billy put happy faces on all the O's in my homework!"

"Don't put me in the deep end!"

"Is this extra-strength pasghetti, Mommy?"

"Mommy looks tired. I'll bet we'll hafta take a nap."

"Dolly! Come here and watch Daddy's face turn red. He's doin' push-ups."

"Every time the President talks, why do a lot of guys hafta come on and tell us what he said?"

"I can't wake up yet. I hafta finish my dream."

"PJ's really smart! He can spell his name."

"Winter is almost over. The ground's pokin' up through the snow."